House At Out

Mark Goodwin

House At Out

*Helen keep
that House At
Out CLEAN!
kind regards
Mark [signature]*

Shearsman Books

First published in the United Kingdom in 2015 by
Shearsman Books
50 Westons Hill Drive
Emersons Green
BRISTOL
BS16 7DF

Shearsman Books Ltd Registered Office
30–31 St. James Place, Mangotsfield, Bristol BS16 9JB
(this address not for correspondence)

www.shearsman.com

ISBN 978-1-84861-418-5

House At Out's Contents

Holy Eke

A ruined room with a river running through the end
of it.

> – Peter Redgrove
> 'The Half-House'
> *From Every Chink of the Ark*

a room for spectacular midnight error

> – Peter Dent
> 'Odd Detail (And Memorandum)'
> *Handmade Equations*

At the road's end you turn round and go back home
but I stand here in acute smallness,

> – Peter Riley
> *Alstonefield*

For three Peters

Holy Eke

a   wild's inf   i   nite b   its
a   house is   fin   ite parts equ

a   lly a   house   &a   wild ef
flo   resce in()finite read(s)ings

exooikos   hole key   exo eco eke echo

Mear Thoon

I

round ground hung   out on
the dark limb   of space
gleaming a tongue of   time & pocks

of in   ner far coiled the   coll
iding of arcs pulls   the twine
of sky into the   ball of dry   sil

ver erosion soon Luna   mind peels
like ship-hull hor   rors & mist
glazes faint rain   bow across hopes

round bow of sin   king hip of a gone
one   our light is taken   from our
bones & held   tight in a disk   of

failing   dimensions the   great de
cay of   love evolves   in air   less dust
moon in a   rid rocks of ago   nised

inst   ruments as music   slips its
other silent self over a   lens and re
leases a back   lit un   known from

the dark round   naught of voice
caught   as rust in the coin or   on
the coin as the cur   rent of months

tugs the wa   fer off   night's tongue

II

wet blue bled deep   on   the globe
skin brown part   icles full   of a
coming al   phabet as the blue tran

slu   cence filled hollows   of god(')s(')
promises the whole   cloud & moist
ure swir   ling voice o   ceans plated

            each   space

with   ever deeper creature designs
the val   leys held blue &   silver thr
eads that fat   tened with fish givings

the soil ut   tered up   its dee
pest de   sires in shapes of gr
een geo   metry & threads of   hyst

erical cellular song   great deserts
held their tongues against the   hot
core of the world as   mountains

whit   ened with water's thin()king
we   hold the bran   ches and feel
the soil bet   ween our toes   we

let salt water   rise & recede
daily thr   ough our own bones
we cup our eye   of a   world with

one heart pum   ping dark void
Earth   has moles bur   rowing
through her to time's   far side

III

round ground hung   out wet blue bled
deep on the dark limb   of space on
the glo   be skin glea   ming a tongue
of brown particles   full of   time & po

cks of inner a coming   alphabet far coiled
the col   liding blue translucence arcs pull
the twin(e) filled hollows of gods   sky into
the ball of prom   ises the whole cloud dry

silver eros   ion moisture's swirling voi
ce the lunar mind peals   ocean plated like
ship-hull   horrors space ever   deeper mist
glazes faint creature   designs rainbow hopes

across valleys h   eld blue &   silver the round
bow of the threads that fattened the sinking hip
of   gone fish givings   the soil one   our light is
taken uttered   up its deepest from   our bones &

held desires in shapes   of green fight in the disk
of geometry threads   of failing dim   ensions dim
ensions the hysterical cell   ular song great deserts
held their gr   eat decay of love tongues   against

the hot evolve in airless   dust the moon in the core
of the world arid rocks of   agonised mountains
whitened instruments   as music thinking of water
we slips its   other silent   self hold   the branches

and feel a lens releases soil   between our toes in
the backlit unknown we   let salt   water rise &
recede daily through the dark round we cup   our
nought of the far voice bones   caught as rust in

the coin eye of world with one   the coin as the heart
pumping dark void currents of   months tug earth
moles burrowing the   wafer time of the far   side

      night's   tongue through her

A Bachelard's Château

hut ancients the   alive   roundhouse existing   lamp
you by the shed   shed light   circle   centre house at
know   house against blows   wind icy while evening

   stills   the roaring stove only to   listen

Our Shoulle

I

grey slates slight   against   raging sky   yet our rain breaks
its back above us   our chimney lets   all our   grey thoughts
escape   and we are left   with the orange-yellow of a   yes
terday   our windows are not   for letting   our light in   but

for keeping our   dark out even   without our curtains   our
glass of our house only allows our   light to be trapped   yet
our house is our lamp   each   of us a filament of our house's

flame   we wait for longing's moth to   flutter   at our windows
so our furniture can creak   its sympathy   for things not done
that could've been   our bricks are red   always even beneath

our grey plaster   our joists   of   our house   once   stood in
our forest   our stone of our house once   rested   in our ground
water passes through our house   via   our cooking & our baths
how our house is taller than our sky it keeps   out our cellar is so

dark   but a beast in it   sings our lullabies

II

a round voice   in   the bottom of an impossible tube   is
nearly silent yet ticks   away   a shiny poem coils   of a
whole other   place pull   me in it is thin in   a last place
a shell makes so wide at first a thrush has smashed   a snail

shell on a doorstep   think   of bricks think   of your family
we always wonder   why sky   doesn't flatten a shell with its
simple vast   coiled solid song song   of wafer stone stone
that is a song a crab may live in   an on & on song   a snail

carries around   exchanges   for size & no size   we do not live
in shells because our feet are too big they would not fit   into a
tight pink compartment   where   a shell goes no   further into
the round of all   a world slates   so slight against her   round

voice bright   raging sky with a rain in a bottom of impossible

III

thoughts escape leave   us free and we are poem   coils
of a whole i am   left   with an orange/yellow other place

pull me in i am   right   without curtains glass is smashed
on a past i am   wrong   part of a flame we are does   not

flatten under dark a simple shell   waits for longing coiled
solid flutters at our round window our furniture   creaks

a song of stone sympathy for things not shell   our bricks
are always red   even beneath a sliding snail our house

once stood where we did not live & where once it did not
the stone of our house is thin shell   because of our bare

17

feet we pass   through our house   via   a tight pink tube
all our cooking & our baths are wall-less   compartments

in a silent   yellow of shell   we are taller than what goes
no further into a round   sky keeping   out all   a   world

Biscuits Thrown From a Window

I

our world's trans   parent mouth takes sigh
t   out of our   livings pace   and fills an out

side with eyes & eye   activity a plane   of
glass holds the fly's journey and   lets light

pass through the bond between heat &   cold
a long view framed by   wood is kept   a

moment   in clear squares then re   leased
to distance & its spat   ial rant   melted sand

is c   lean and magnifies or shr   inks or b
ends   the sun's warmth as seen   or not we

stare out of the wind   o   it takes us from our
corner but leaves us   with   our bodies it

takes our seeing in   to the vast as   we sit
or stand in our   cell the air   pushed through

an open window curtains billowed like two
people fattening & starving & fattening &

starving ...   and so it was   food began to fall
through a/the win   dow in a/the form of   un

seen dreams   a square dream clearly fitted
perfect   ly between bits of processed tree

II

wheat tightened to dry   tiles or discs of food
a biscuit crumb   bles a valley of corn harvest
and its she   aves are c   rushed to crumbs

each   dry moon cru   shed by teeth yields calor
ies like ferv   our for   a belief of going   on in a
body the bisc   (yo)u   it man with f   rail bones

of down ground & cooked grains very carefully
led his life away from rat   tling jolts or damp
cell   ars the field I played in as a child   with

its gol   den   stubble fresh after   the combine
sits on my table as a small circle I can put my
mouth   round I watch   the g   olden light on

biscuit change as a biscuit   sun sinks into hedge
row each crumb from what   I've crunched cool
ing amongst dust   and it's   lost to the ants as to

kens of civilisation they   take each token back
to the nest   where   calories for momentum are
stored for the long   distance & time   it takes

to evolve to   a moment of inventing biscuits

III

see   -through wheat world's   mouth takes sight   out
of food-discs living   space   crumbles a valley of corn

outside eyes   ' sheaves   glass holds dry   moon crushed
by   teeth let light   pass threw   to yield bonds between

heat &   belief   in a body of moment   a long view   in
clear ground-down & cooked   grains coins   then released

to very care   fully lead   my life bend   sun's warmth with
golden stubble as seen   or not we   after combines stare

out of   a window my table   as a small circle takes   us
from our   corner I   can put my mouth round   hosts our

seeing into a biscuit's change   vast as I sit whilst biscuit
sun sinks stand   in our cell's air hedgerow   each   crumb

pushed through open from   what I've crunched   collects
people fat   ten   ing &   starving tokens   to the ants   civil

ization's window forms un   seen calories   a square dream
stored for round   distance clearly   fitted perfectly between

times it takes to   evolve bits   of processed tree frame our
c   lear moment of in   venting biscuits as pains   of glass con

                    f   use f   lies

wilder by stars
houseless hinge

      read empty

chrysalis cold
passing remains

Bhaormne

I

a door-bang in wind   hay-ghosts stacked on oak   whiffs
of cow & horse sorts   whiffs   of dust & smudged light
gliding through slat-gaps   gather   in a gone &   come

gather in specks of outside   straw & grain   bundles of
light   store   a blood of days in a wooden heart   (in come
field-riches   out   go fragments of food)   keep light dry

under a high roof   a barn begins   where endings are snapped
& draped & stacked   amongst   a leaking of light into a barn
a chicken picking for crystals in dust   swallows   in mud-

hands that grasp rafters   swallows in mud-huts upside down
a barn throbs in a red light   oak beams ring & resound with
past's saps   a barn is a lap is a door   ajar   is a flapping   yet

      still   in a wind where we begin

II

on her sofa   on her back   staring   at home-parts   fragments
of fractal love   tiny homes within a home   home's vast   vast's
home   she at ease to be knickerless or she may be dressed   in
her best histories   a tiny child's voice heavy and polished in floor

boards   a glint   of barn in her home's shine a   conversion for
eternal cargo   her hearth   holds   out its hot   hand   her hearth
holds a jewel of fire   gleams through humans   a voice of her tiny
child glitters on   edges   of ornaments that mean   a handshake &

a kiss in her doorway   cold beyond savoury smells within   she
stares at her ceiling   sugars   are painted through its fascinating
cracks   her house holdholds an old barn's cargos   a greenery of
home-air   a plant life unfurls from root to roof   its eatableness   her

home-food that feeds her sighs   makes   them fat with song   a ling
ering within   a home's moment   a lengthening   of a second years
ago   a smell   that makes a roof that bars time's rain yet   allows
space   to patter into her nostrils'   caves   into her brain's castle to

impregnate her untouchable   soul's walls

III

a hearth holds door-bangs for wind   ghosts
of hay stack jewels of fire   cow-breath glows
through humans   a tiny child's voice sorts

whiffs of horses   smudged light on   edges

of dusty ornaments   a kiss in a doorway gathers
in come & gone   specks   of outside are cold
beyond   light is kept dry within sugars   a house

hold of cracks stores the blood of days   riches

from fields stare at parts of home   a barn begins
a tiny home   within   a vast castle   she is knick
erless as endings snap   a child leaks light into

histories   a chicken picks heavy voices   from

floorboards   crystals in dust have a soft certain love
a barn throbs song   oak beams ring   a sound of a
second years ago   a smell that makes a roof of past's

saps   a door that bears time's rain   nostril-wind

      breath is where we begin

aching breath
souls begin along feet

landscape growth across
tiny walk

cloud printed along moment

Doors in Woods

brambles mouth pillows

a person's steps
break brown hearing

from wind's signature

branches bark agreements
accept through mould

a thrush-shape

•

through animal-bed

heaviest mouth-skills
& eyes ceiling a door

•

tongues elongating
through brambles

crackling plays
of ice

broken hearing
sheds strangers' feet

feet rip against
cross-hatch

gathering reminders

•

moss passing
the room

woven tongues
gate sense's

dreams from brambles

•

reading mouths'
seasons opens slats

open slats smell
mushroom

an asocial
nostril blurs

•

closed wood(-)shapes
gather a thrush

brambles' skills
zip eyes

stories become
one ring

of woven hair

•

vast abyss-doors
warm nothing

gold stories
beam people

through toes

travel is
the hole

builders feather

•

corner pushing
through woven dream

woods amongst
clothed crunch

liquid creeks
become a bed's

signature

•

in step hear
ling & sea

ever-sensitive
twigs can open

cross-mush
in some

croaked mind

•

cracks passing loss

forgotten eyes
meeting ceilings

the heaviest hole
pockets

human shapes

band in doll shapes take bone

beetle thoughts
scratchy

star bone
fast brown
shit shouts

four trees' nails

Woods In Room

I

winter woods pull   a person's   figures in
amongst moss -clothed tall ones   a step
on a crunch of broken solar   moments hear

ing is crisp readings of brown crack   ling
mouths shed   from intricate plays all   sea
sons lose to tongues   of ice & wind's ever

-elongating signature passing through sens
itive   branches to   pick up bits   of twig
&   bark brambles   are agreements feet can

not accept where trousers may   rip against as
one who is lonely pulls   their mouth of open
tasting through rough closed   slats & cross

-hatch a smell   of wood-mould &   mush
room shapes an asocial gath   ering in some
human nostril a   thrush blurs   to crooked

& twig   gy()re   minders

II

a lit   standing lamp & its   corner hold
dry gold liquid of passing stories & the
creak of beams that could become people

if the   one in   the room thought through
rings   & grain toes on wo   ven animal
hair feel traces of   travel placed   a bed

stead   is a crane that will   lift the heaviest
dream from the hole   of a human mouth
and the pillows are bags of old forgotten skills

builders zipped into each   feather two eyes
stare at three cracks meeting   on a ceiling
and passing away across the vast loss of a

ceiling's so   lid abyss it is   only the door
& its   pockets of knowledge & its   two
sides one warm the other   cold that makes

nothing an offering

III

win   ter woods pull at a standing-
lamp man figures   in amongst corn

ers of dry   golden li   quid moss
-clothed tall ones step on passing

stories'   creeks on the crunch of
broken beams that could be   come

solar moments hearing   people of The
one crisp reading(s) of   brown room

thought through rings crin   kling
mouths shed from g   rain toes woven

seasons lose animal   hair tongues
of ice & wind's t   ravel placed The

bed   crane is an ever   -long gate
-signature   passing through sensitive

branches will lift the heaviest dream
pick   up bits of bark   & twigs from

the hole of a   human pillows &
mouths in agreement with brambles

feet can't accept   old forgotten kills
trousers may rip   against built   zips

into   each as one who   is lone   ly
pulls their feather 2 eyes stare mouTh

open ta   sting through three cracks mee
ting rough closed slats & cross-hatch

ceiling passing away a smell   of wood
-mould in a vast loss of ceilings(') mush

rooms shape solid   abyss an a   social
gathering of doors in pockets of doubt

a human nostril & a Th   rush with its two
sides blurs   of twiggy reminder & oTher

cold make Thing a   No!   of fur & ring

blackened solid spikes
birch dark like organised notion

animal vibrated sound
wings rub cathedral

deep tiny gongs

Or Tomb

an autumn beech begins   all branch
ness to trap and house   and home

and hone a   mind of sky-leaf sheets
lamp   ness of being   at   spattered

or greased across a catering   for far
space & in   clean greens & bleeding

oranges over   lap   flakes in layer-say
ing with   light the silent word   *light*

a light word   the silence of the word
light is how gleam   is   hiss as is glisten

whisper the year's   tilt is collecting   in
glassy senses leaves   vibrate neural mat

rix spiked by spark   thoughts that beech
tree's long green dark lengths smooth as

kiss & ice-poli   shed rock r   each   thr
ough fantasy's glances   to pull actuals

from   shallow vast   into deep leaf-lit
place an   in-here with   in hearing   put

a hand on   cold bark and pull   put a foot
in a crux   and push   smelling a green

that paints   clothes & skin as a someone
slither-climbs autumn   awetumn's each

each separate   each each   click of a leaf's
disconnecting each   soft clatter of fall each

gentle con   necting clunk to ground re
leases travel's & arrive's entwinings un

wind lets leaves of selves &   of others of life
who all tilt to   wards moist ground of gone

one day dead where   a beech tree's great plate
root cath   edral curl-drilling in dark grains' in

feeds the leaf   -light the lovely   greens &
oranges of beech leaves back   lit is Di   wali

by day & if poe   try was blind   beechs' written
woods would let light be   heard   stated with

a green leaf turn   ing rust in a   mouth this

is is   is a

sunlight across   *me*
rhododendrons button   *think*

so (growing on white)

lost den is birdbath of   *nothing*
souls pigeon   *I'd*

Old Tone

translated from   Peter Dent's *New Register*

smoking   old reds leaving all their others
for winter vales when her one hears   if
instant   calm from an axle of full ground

her sounds   less similar for straight poverty
her slow tarnished organism   and her contract
reply to every besides   she believes she believes

herself a request honest by when   hearing under
vales what sounds like ease   ground drowning
down from betray   strange troubled tracks then sure

possible to write   she'll be starting so troubling
her moonchart right to day   for lust right fully
fulfilled   just a material reality giving up

on hearing her on and plus knowing   its trouble as
moving a permanent register   questions slooshing out
from a synthetic river   gone January demolished

answering to hear her in   shrubs low in the vale
lose her reasoning down the marvellous   peripheries
of certainty   she's driving murky set she's for come

Moving

I. Moving Stillness

from here   to   speech &
by a   liquid   on a rock
slipping electric   ally along
a wheel's revolution films
frames   blur & pull an
eye   sleepily or speedily
into & out of the   fast
clouds slipping along distance
& through space   we   wheel
along our   journey
packing the contents of
our house to   move   to
the next   life &   a world's
emotions   boil   in a
mouth & spurt   from
lips to swirl   out then   in
to an ear & another world's
motions   of fear   or
peace or lust emerge
from   another   mouth fast
& swirl   into   another's
ears & so   a speech
moves into another's speech

hare   under dog's   stare
frozen as grass   cased
in ice we are   still   here
here is still an owl's
still   shadow   still an owl's
shadow molecules gripped
in crystal   chains air
thick   as glass   granite sat
on ground   patient   as
nowhere clenched in gone
stare at the rock &   the
look that bangs   back   at you
is stillness   your body grinds
as cold invades soft
with   solid old   space
in the   sky has   collapsed
& the battle is   over with
its horrible   silence & the
snap of   light   on film
the grip of   image the
imprisonment of rush
flow   captured jagged
unchangeable sounds   a

and a voice   moves through
another's voice &   longing
or hating are   arranged
in   motion so   a music
is   felt as time   moves
outside a cage of   gone's not

melody with   out time an
impossible   song without   seconds
or minutes the   absolute
zero of a   god's   grave in
the still dark   of   space a hard
hole of   iced lightless silence

II. Moving Conversions

a mouth spurts   solid old   space words
convert movements to   words   a mouth
sucks liquid-new   substance inspiration

       replaces still

•

a swirl into another's   imprisonment   of rush
a cage whose bars are   speed & change   a
whoosh of a lock's   tumblers a lover's   fall

     into a bound   less   boxed other

•

another's voice longing   impossible   song with
out seconds or minutes a voice   moving through
melody without   time   hating arranged minutes'

  absolutes loving moving   without   space

•

a wheel's revolution films   here's   still owl to
slip revolt there's owl's   soundless   flight plays

headlights & sh   utter -whirr attempt   capture
now's owl's sudden   ghostly   swoop   cuts

the engine ticking   over   after crash then's
slow   motions   of final   scenes   move   on

•

along our journey nowhere   clenches   gone so
yesterday   will   move slowly away   I try to
imagine flying birds without   motion   so I am

   close   to our time without its space

•

another's speech moves un   changeable sounds
another's speech changes unmov   able sounds
another's speech   sounds   unmovable changes

speech -sounds move   a   changeable other
speech -moves   change   another's sound
changed speech   others   a sound-move chang

   ed sound-moves speak another

•

as time moves   the   still dark of   space
our earth spins whilst   the   flowing dark
face of earth trickles through human fingers

•

clouds slip along distance   thick   as glass
the ground   near   to my feet rushes   past
I cannot stand still   as   the world turns be

   neath this sky's hot lens

●

through space   we   wheel on ground   our
ground wheels through space   we rough heels
pace round   go   eels race through our ponds
will we   grace   our round peals   our ploughs
turn earth   our planet   revolves   through

       space we wheel on ground

●

emotions boil as cold invades soft
lovers in ice move through minds

as the still zero settles its   halo
what was told hot unfolded fast

●

eyes sleep   ily & speed   ily shadow molecules
sight follows particle   logic   virtual skin feels

a trickle of electrons as sweat   down   a spine

●

frames blur and   pull still
shadows   a movie-maker
melts stills   across   eyes

●

from here to   speech   a hare under dog's stare
from yelp to race   a child's flowing   tears

from   blood   to soul   a story being   told
from here   to then   is   then to   there

from   sniff to poem   a   man's hunger from
here to speech   a hunted to hunting   beast

•

in   motion a zero
of a god's   grave

we bury self   in
a   still centre of

    change

•

into   & out of fast crystal chains   a per
petual solution as perpetual   solid stuck
fast to   speed   a perpetual motion   a

computer   flick -flacks zeros &   ones
a chemist in a lab   just   realising the in

    stant of blast

•

lips swirl the sky has collapsed a kiss
of wind speaks flying debris   puffed
cheeks   and then   a tongue's arrow

bang on target   down   a voice-box
a vortex   roaring in a world's throat

•

our house   to move to   with solid old   space
where reverie is   so   solid &   young with its

    flowing

•

outside is   gone's   hole of iced light
less silence   inside is   arrival's whole

            melted bright   sound

•

peace & lust emerge   fast from a mouth
quick-touch   hatches   its tongue warm

    -voiced loose   movements   spill

•

the next   life a world's
snap of   light on   film

a celluloid body revolved
projects   its sexy ghost

•

slipping   electrically   along on ice
we are still here in our speed   though

the electric whiz of ice on skin seems
to burn us see   -through slipping quicker

as our slope deepens trees   tangle fast
enings & dances in   blur   our fingers

meet   electricity moves through with us
moves through   us   moves us   arrival

            & moving have merged

•

the next life   &   the world are
stillness your   body   grinds this
life & a heaven is movement your

        soul breathes

•

a   speech's flow   captured
jagged but   we makers heat
each   icicle-syll   able till it

        melts

water denying wasp
predictably unlike green leaves

don't bud the will

Sast Flow

I

trees stretch the   ir widths across   my face as my
heart pumps footpath through   my mind tunnel

ling my foot is slid   ing on a kerb my hand whips
a twig glass glints   like   a tin   y star in a smud

ge of place ch   ange I am speed's   doll I am being
that is emp   tied & fil   led at once by shapes hurt

ling past me and through my   eyes I   take a next
bend with a soul's acc   eleration I feel a bone elon

gate along a second's del   usion the railings along a
rail   way line clatter as my breath bursts   on each The

treeline constell   ation of twigs & leaves mi   grates ac
ross a milli   onth of nothing as my body slides the rind

of exi   sting not here not there yet   bet   ween a slot
of tra   velling melts   with space and dissolves a glea

ming line along my fing   ernail

42

II

t   his next mill   imetre is a grime trance a chip
of granite h   olds a my's perception like water
slowly free   zing sunsh   ine goes   on   dro

pping photon aft   er phot   on on   -to a vast p
atch of a squ   are inch a my's tiny shad   ow craw
ls over a range of pollen grains   it was last y   ear

writ   ten on a pine need   le's edge that reminded
a me of the spee   d lost along a fol   ded & bent way
an I can   smell each trick of dust at (t)his altitude ten

(s)cent   imetres above grass now a mi   cron a glea
ming oil slick on tarm   ac wastes stretch away
(fr()om a me man()y mes)   & near in on convo

luted loss of dis   tance a my's hands scrape over grit
an I drag   s my skin for one century over (t)he star
t & end of e   very journey never made a little cow in

a small bag graz   ing on mem   oriesisafirstofamy's
fantasies to attack amewithacongealedmo(o)   vement
&acurlingstillnessjustnotstillgrazingitslayersthrough

a place not crossed

III

this n   ext millim   etre is a grime tree's stretch
their wid   ths next the chip of granite holds acr
oss my face as my trance heart pumps footpath

perception like wa   ter slow   ly through my mi

nd tunnelling fr   eezing sunshine goes on drop
ping my foo   t sliding on a photon after photon on
to a vast   kerb my hand whips   a patch of square

43

inch my tiny twig glass glints like a shadow crawls

over a range ti   ny star in a sm   udge of pollen
grains it was last place change   I am year written
on a pine needle speed doll I   am being edge *that*

reminded me of That   emptied & filled speed lost

along *the* folded at once by   A shape's hurt & bent
way I can smell each ling past me and through track
of dust at this alt   i   tude my eyes take the next ten

centimetres above the grass b   end with a soul's ax

-now a micron above a gleaming elleration I feel A
bone o   il sli   ck on tarm   ac the wastes elongate
along a sec   ond's stretch away & near inon delu

sion railings along convol   uted loss of distance my

railway line cl   atter as hands scr   ape over grit m
y breaths burst a century   I drag my   skin for one
treelineconstellationoverthestarendofevery   twig

& leaves migrate across jour   ney never made a mill

ionth of n   o   thing as little cow in a small   bag my
body slides rinds of grazing on memories is   exi(s)t
ing   not here not   there is the first of my fantasies

between a slot attack   me with a congealed of trave

lling mel   ts with space m   ovem   ent and a cur
ling sti   ll dissol   ves a gleaming ness just hot still
grazing its layers through a p   lace line along my fin

gern   ail not crossed

tree derelict stops her
suddenly oak dark mists remember

myth's tree balanced

winter is rented in twigs

it is inter & beyond   it is peal
light whitely crisp on air bright
as moments gone   sadness is
clink   an icicle of thinking grown
through soul   a last star blinks
on a blanket   caught by frost's
cloth   a little girl speaks   a
brittle voice of mist   rabbits
foxes a long time ago   in the

solidity of zero

meadow moment
rattles child

built pool throws still blown

Fice

I

ion flight cracks open air   blue-orange wriggle
-lightening   wood-will pulled down to grey   heat's

speech pours   up   out of sacrifice   heat's heart
of points pushes smoke vowels   away   a scream

of hot space   tugs   at bones   bones as a basket
of fire cradles a soaked lady sailor   steam hisses

a snake's   demise   fire's teeth begin a meal   sparks
fowl throat   flames inside wrists   black-letter-bones

under   twirling coloured-paper flames   she is heat's

II

cold congeals clear   skins a lake with window
an icicle tooths air   a crack of sun is held   in

a gun of icicle   his finger bones of clear raging
ache   a coil   of ice water-glued to a dead tree's

wood   each   coil of ice   part   of a jacket of
light & frozen possibilities   a sparkle of captured

light   a ring of escaping   sound light   suffices
as ice impels   a glacier collapses into gone's heart

ice at dusk   blue-black wisps of never   loneliness
visibly solid   ice's smell super-metallic & precisely

vast

III

crack open air   clear congeals cold in air's
speech sun is held   dead-wood-lightening pulled
through a lake's solid window as heat   pours

out of vowels   smoke & heat's sacrifice c   lear
raging   aches a scream of   space jackets light
her bones basket possibilities   a sparkle of

captured cradles a lady's glacier in gone's heart
she is heat's wisps of   nothing   her black letters
papery-cold make solidity lonely   flames twirling

colours in coils of ice

wind through cloth
wind creaks

        digesting trees

memories' solution
erupts stinking house

Ape Saint Planderc

an old man's colourless   voice paint   spent
across space a bleed of brushing emerges from

a dot at a   left edge of a morning   stranded
in colour & an after   noon thinking in frames

a limit to point & pointing all   defied   now

        then young

•

land   scape glass tongues all lick   thoughts of four
walkers on the brow of a world it was not   blue or
green or brown that tortured one walker it was a gold

speck in a drop of   water a speck   engraved with a
little picture of a cottage &   lambs it was torture to feel
a glint on   his eye was a blade of   glass a green   blade

of glass amongst millions that spelt a   gony across a face
of a second walker and a third walker an explorer   used
to ice & temperature(')s well   below ethics was tormented

by a 'the' thrush's radio tuning in to a 'the' middle distance
a whirling beauty pulleyed wires   from his heart connected
to a 'the' sky the 'a' sky of glass tongues all licking at four

talkers'   'the' oughts their talking   like a tube of acrylic
stamped on a glint of agony & gleam   of release or()bit
a mess as land   below slow   ly dissolves in a walk of four

beg   innings' unableness

•

painter begs in by   look & then   finishes
a it   with then's   first straight black   line
a painter   answered a door in   a 'a' colourful

way a sign   of lines she was a great painter
who found the last point of gold on a crawling
ant's back   it   is possible to be   a painter

and never use   paint the blank   canvas of a
year will be stretched   tight as a second   he was
a painter when young as a green shoot in old age

painting crept   across his face to   dried crinkly
sent   iments it is not always   possible to finish
a painting but it is oneway possible to paint   a fin

ishing's   loss a look was pul   led from a painter's
eye a black line look yanked out by blank   she
& he as pain   t fell in love as deep as a sp   lodge

of golden black

•

49

landscape gloss tongues begin a painter's   look lick
thoughts of four & then finish with then's walkers on

a brow of a first straight black line world   was not blue
a painter answered one tortured   walker was a door in

a colourful way   on a colour()ful(l) way   in colour's
way she was   a gold speck in a dropped   sign of lines

she was of   water a speck engraved   a great painter
with a little picture of a found last point   cottage & lambs

gold on an ant's crawling torture   to feel a 'the' glint in
gold his eyes   were the 'a' blade of possible to be   point

a green blade and never use   paint glass amongst million's
black canvas of a year spelt a gone   stretched tight explore

used to ice a green   shoot temperatures   well below age
painting across face a thrush   's radio tuning faeces & dried

crinkly sentiments in middle   distance it   is not always
possible it is   not always possible to   swirl beauty pulled

wires finish a   painting a sky finishing   loss a glass tongue
was pulled from a painter   four walkers' eyes a black line

some look of thoughts talking is like a tube of look pulled out
by blank acrylic stamped   on a she & he as painters felled

a glint of   gone & glee   in love as deep as The Land Peace
orbits   a splodge of gold   a land below slowly   black

empty quarry ark lit
in nest a darkness knotted

tent unseen

homemade with splashed rasps
pale woodland rant

Windscreen Book

where any dark refrain may overload the real – Peter Dent

trees reiterate all texts' bits   especially   winter-opened
twig-elaborate   with twilight's purpler/blacker to wood

with car-slide & pass -us-by fibres   *here*   an angle of
A   oak-curl Ss & Cs   Christ's T   cross-criss runes   ash

-Arabics   black/white birch-Chineses   *there*   with a sky
patient for dark scratches of before-voice   none-semantics'

sensing of make   of to make   out of world & in   world &
through   mind & out   for soul   like this patch on blank

of   lines/(curves)/lines   are more   than *than*

hand map intricate
to the skirtingboard

her rid splinter

man happening
down his cave

Bowaterok

I

page crinkles   black pulls   flicker   your finger traces
spaces   between leaves   white/black inside   brown door
covering book   clean & old smell   stare   a black/white

matrix wriggle   on you   into you   you   can slip into

letters   let   yourself sink beyond   crisp print into paper's
vast deep millimetres   your light squashed   into black ink
bleeds   paper's white nought   drips lengthening to trickle …

II

… plop pluhf splat   water talk over rock   smear   like idea
of soul   water-kisses   of water on water   trickles expand
accelerate to rills   rivulets & least   resistance   clear silver
clear gold   pools of clear distance   liquid of aim   ripples

catch eyes   and stare   back somewhere forgotten   surface
tension   deflects & lets   cuddle-waves   water wears a way
wears a permanence of change   gleams   a constant garment
never staying   page crinkles sound pulls   black makes …

III

… pools   or some rivers of other   talk traces spaces water   over
rock between leaves   water on book in water   thin garment on

ground   book-smells of clean old   wet sometimes else some

wear together can tension   cuddles with waves read   rivulets of
least resistance   wriggle in you glint of pages   of water turning

soaked   leaves like love indefinable

tilt dead cathedral leaf

rebreak place upon knolls
afraid land's stones selves later

full roadside's chrysalis corner

road's surface home's house

ghylls walking before   drought   pushing reeds out
a few sex maniac boys   right standing   do suspect

the moon   soil fraction walking   under moisture &
moisture   & moisture   seam-picker tracks   sticking

our compasses   sun pins   pumps   sketching ivy
roots   lazy gold   standing youthful feet   up from

fill

translated from Harriet Tarlo's *becks running after*

the snake begins hand
her mouthing rope of gleams

hammer the attentions
evening slides wit

his clacked ladder her song

Meeting at Hunger Hut

a white hut's chimney bleeds   soot   talk as
mud-flats wait   for sea-speak across estuary

cranes   pick at horizon & dry   grasses make
faint yellow squeals   an African's face sealed

over bone brings   a chipped moon to this hut
so   in the fireplace moon glows as   African

soot sings to sky   a docker with a coat woven
from ink & a stare   full of distance   slips his

shadow through the hut's door like   print that
fell from a pen   and so   breasts   as coinage a

naked gold lady with a spear of molten   writing
writhes over mud   flats towards the white   hut

cradling two dead   an horizon's cooling   towers
add cloud to heaven as sun   light electrifies   the

hut's white skin finally   sea slips over mud like a
choir as solid   gold smiles melt in the fire   place

55

wind open distant talk
clouds corn's air

golden earth's
dryness in furrows

parcel soft graves

Hoght Liuse

I

ho!   use is all   floors & walls of a per   son's
birth the street   & field outside fit   into each

window times   over also   wrap bricks with
near & distant   sounds the stairs   & wardrobe

crush   in on an a   lone space & bring   out
gleams of hiding   the roof   is at a star   t of

distance and wears   itself like a hat   each tile is
the silk punch on a pia   no made of a child breath

ing in some nursery kitchen   smells squiggle
through air and up   the chimney to   1976 at 1976

the whole house col   lapses   into a party of play
ers in the drawers   fighters in the clocks begin

to clean a house with the   999 id   eas each idea
is   soft but pre   cise by   a time   a house has

been a home for three families   the shine on
each house-syllable projects the faces & breaths

of all the private dramas the house presented to
the audience of its   self a house   at   an end

of a   street has big   windows made from cat
-bones & river-   water slip   into the house via

                    the back-tree

II

light squ   eezes through   openness its   efforts
make vast wheeze like a   god's   problem voice

solving a blank whole of the no   thing   light a
cross earth pulls plants into th   oughts   reach

beams of light over   water wrestle   with neon bones
under water   moon's light sp   ends itself into a well

the sound of light at night is sweeter than the bittering
of   sun the jet   of photons tight as ice cuts   the dark

mind   open the halves   of dark mind are hot with
the blade   gleam animals   grow from the division

the awakening of light was caused by Mrs Black
switch   ing the soot in   her he   art her   new

soot met   with Mr Black's he   at & the fuse   of
possibility hurt   o   ever so   much the long finger

of light feels through tree   tops and ploughs wet
grass and scrapes   over rock mountain tops   un

til it   points to a whole in a sky   where   no
finger points   back but   a god's not being his   ses

with a go   ddess's laser

III

house is all floors &   walls light   squeezes
through the   street's openness – its effort makes

a person's   birth the field   outside fits into
each vast god problem   voice solving the window

many times over wrap the bricks   with near nothing
distant   sounds The   stairs & light across Earth's

pull wardrobes   crush in on the light alone   spaces
bring out the plants into thought's reach   gleams

of hiding   roof beams of light   over water at the
start distance wrestles with neon   bones a silk

punch spends itself a piano   made from the sound
of   light a child   breathes kitchen night   sweeter

smells squiggle through sun bittering up the chimney
jet photons tight as ice at 1976   the whole house cuts

the dark mind open   party halves of dark   mind
players in the drawer are hot with the   blade the clock

begins gleam   animals grow   999 cleans the house
with division   each idea is awakening light soft but

precise by the   caused   Mrs Black switching   time the
house   has been the soot in   her heart her home

for three families' new soot met with Mr She   shine
on each house blacks   heat the fuse   syllable projects

the faces of possibility hurt over the breaths of all the
private light feels through   tree the house   presented

ploughs through   wet   the audience of itself grass
scrapes over   rocks the house   the end of the mountain

tops until it streets big   windows point to the whole
made from cat-bones & sky where no finger points river

water slip   into the back of   God's not   being house
via the back   tree hisses   with Goddess's laser

feels through over

IV

somelight   house is
all walls &   floors

light squeezes through
a   person's birth

fits   each into vast

a   sea-distance solves
a   window   many

times   over

horizon   sounds
bring   out

thought's lit   reach
dark   halves of minds

on sea   collapse
a smell   through air

use   is all
for   safe

song through sea
today's escape

pulled selves
cold as centre

begin choir
of bronze

Environmental Taster

reflection   on a painting's glass   bright
window-light through   which to lower

legs a moment   like a gas in a box   then
gone   a track   sinks into ground green

door with   PULL   written we raise our
ears for floors   go   up as sky a   figure

pulling a hill across skin into one joy we
are always   exclaiming when   earths met

he framed the moves'   obvious foreground
she framed the hut   into one despair we

despise a planet   shrinks   going up its
chimney   can't I hear a knife swimming

within hearts   can't you say   the corners
rushing to free our hand   shakes from breath

61

tiny corner to audience
interior the split theatre's gesture

arguments tremble
straight with abyss

Flattened Shop

a bird's   sweet painted   flight on tin
cherry blossom & fat   orange sun

a blue-bird smacked   against glass
nine green tins with all   China's dynasties

collapsed within   shelved dust -free
faces kissing glass   leave   no grease or mist

a grid   of wooden boxes for food -stuffs
taste   less as cool repeatedly cleaned   glass

vibrations   of rummaging musk   try & try
behind panes' gleaming silence   we reflect

rat & mouse-traps   snapped   tight on shadow
fine   flattened creatures rinsed see -through

that carry no disease and   are   as genuine as
believed   smack against glass   and pass

through

Sboo Udly

I

ghost   swirled fast & bright in   a contained vast a
ringing grind of va   pour rubbing untouched again

st bricks window frames millions of miles off on a
world at other   end of black tube each lit   click to

night is   the cut voice of a   soul a cut voice of the
soul a soul   of voice cut all   the stars are one soul's

last smashed perhaps   real   music scoots across a
glass surface of soul-eye seen shapes of else   where

dissolve   on an in   terface of soul-control   a whole
soul-network re-boots as   shadow casts more   dark

spooks through a bright light at the end of a telephone
a wire is a being craw   ling through tight surprise(d)

it   is my soul in your   eye-gleam that is in   danger
of falling   out in   to grass to be drowned   in a rain

drop let soul   slip to river to ride nothing's currents

II

skin is sk   y-feet stretched over bone of hoping in
ground a sound   of skin is a shush a   gentle skid

of sound over a surface of   being a framed structure
that carries my flesh &   sense is   not separate from

sky I keep   pieces of   sky in my   lungs always and
my feet have the whole ploughed & wild earth stuck in

each tiny can   yon of print swir   ling on the bottom
of a   toe a first body I   found that fitted me was made

from animal flav   ours I walked around in a taste   of
creature wrapped in meals of meat I cooked myself in

the sun it was   then that   my body cracked open now
like a bread   loaf a sound   of speaking was sick   on

a floor of ru   shing beetles each   named Gregor

III

ghost swir   led fast skin sky st   retched brigh   t
in a con   tained   vast over   the bone of hoping

the r   inging grind of in   ground vap   our rubbing
untouched sound sk   in against bricks a shush   a

gentle skid window fr   ames mil   lions of sounds
over surface world at   the other end-structure t   hat

carries of a black   tube each my flesh   & sense 1   it
click to   night is the not   separate I keep   pie   ces

of cut voice of a   soul sky all   st   ars are   one sky
in my lungs' always my feet   have the last smashed

souls perhaps real   music whole ploughed and wild
earths stuck in each gloss   surface scoots across a

soul-eye of seen cany   ons of print shapes of   else
where dissolve swirls   on the bottom on   the inter

f   ace of soul a toe   the first body control the   whole
soul I   found that fit   ted   me net   work re-boots a

soul made from an   imal shadows   cast more dark
flavours I walk around spo   ok through the bright in

the taste of crea   ture light at the end wrapped   up in
meals the telephone   wire is of meat I then cooked a be

ing crawling through myself in the s   un it was that my
tight surprise in   my soul your   eye-body cracked o

pen gleam that is   in danger a loaf of bread falling out
into   the   grass the sounds   of speaking to drowned

in a raindrop was   sick on the floor let   souls slip to riv
er rushing beetles ride nothing's cur   rents each named

Greg   or

will wardrobe release reflection
footpath every reflection veil
off wardrobe

footpath with our soul separation

Gowl Un

I

an owl gow   n h   anged in dar   k cloud-bran

ches glow   ers a hoot of o   ther sound's sides
while wild feather-flutter fing   ers a flight's

silence claws   of solid air scritch   across a fur
ry   face light from a moon face   rotates direct

ional erot   icisms all spok   en in eye gl
int clinks cough   balls of house   -parts dissolve

in the tur   bid but moon   -illu   minated pond at
the forest's   throat the screech   of owl lung sad

ness hangs   out flapping conc   epts on a white
line of star   -stretch the mouse   in black grasses be

low itching black branches w   here two eyes &
skull-covered   feathers stare feels   a razor of breath

flip its   bones & a nest   of fluf   fy magi
cians with yolk   y ass   istants begin stripping syl

lables & dichoto   mies from a rodent's fading
skeleton last   night an   owl's soul exp   anded

and clatte   red softly across a million ferns & mosses

II

a trig   ger of gold is   touched by a light fin
ger of old bent barrel forces   a bullet's grim   ace

across breast-bones   gleam the hand   grabs a cold
metal organ and pumps   a life's dredge sense of

rotating   ch   amber of silent   sayings hard as
myth's disin   tegrating tipped   by skull am

bitions each slee   ping gun in the war   drobe snores
a smoke of stories   the wake   ful gun snif   fing

its way   through a soul   -parade opens
fire and in   side fire all   the heat of gods'

grief expands   in an in   stant of eyes & bone
pain is not going   to kill a gun's   aim pain the

barrel riffles as silver   scrat   ches cause a life's sp
in to craze across grief's smoo   th surface a pool

of gun-blo   od a dying   gun a crowd of frigh
tened   guns & a gun's   mother weeping gold &

sold (golden souled) bull   ets down steel cheeks

III

an owl-gown   hanged in a trigger of gold dark
cloud branches   glower touched by a light
finger a hot of other sounds   on old bent barrel

forces sides while wild feather bullets a grimace
across flut   ter-fingers a flight's breast-bone
gleam the hand grabs   a cold silence claws   of

solid air sc   ritch across a metal organ furry face
light from a life's   dr   edge a moon   face
rotates a rotating   chamber dire   ctional erotic

isms all silent saying hard spoken   in eye
glint clinks myths   disintegrate cough balls
of house   parts tipped by skull   ambitions' each

sleeping gun   dissolves in the turbid but moon
-illuminated pond at the wardrobe snore   by fo
rest's   throat the smoke   of stories wakeful

        gun sniffing screech   owl lung

sadness way through a soul-parade hangs out   fl
apping concepts opens   fire   & inside fire on wh
ite line of star   stretch the mouse in all   the heat

of gods the black grass   below grief expands itching
black branches were instants   of eyes & bone two
eyes & skull covered pain not going   to kill a gun's

aim feather stares   feel   a razor the barrel   riffles
as silver breaths flip bone   a nest of magician's
scratches cause a life with yolky   assistants begin

spin to   craze across stripping syllables   & grief's
smooth surface a pool of gun   blood & dichotomies
from a rodent's last   night a dying   gun a crowd

a fad()ing   skeleton and owl's soul expanded off
frightened   guns a gun's mother wee   ping gold
clattered softly across a million   ferns & mosses &

sold bul   lets down st   eel cheeks

hoot flutter solid
moon spoken house

light grimace grabs sense

from Two that Accidentally Polish A Reflection
translated from Laura Riding's *For One Who Will Dust*   *a*   Shadow

give   in our sleek reflection for its wardrobe   on the
evening hardly comb it more   you release it and   arrive

our soul clothed without yes   reflection to strip   but
press our large soul from its footpath   on the evening

then you've stripped it   out every careless innumerable
obstacle now   push a sleek reflection off certain   at mid

night it will be lost   detesting a veil off our thigh   exist
in dawn   a lot sly   way our reflection off a sky   and

on day push close   our reflection for its wardrobe that is
full   partly night   but far off its large footpath   stands

our energised large soul to be muddied with hunger   if
you give these eases exactly enough   to strip our ego

out   in the roundabout guess   now you & our soul & our
sleek reflection will   all strip   in loud varied separation

with everything right above

Persect in Son

I

hung   in the frame   of clothes trouser-aligned &
shirt held   a voice to make   lungs leak out to or lock
with world often a hat   is ringing a skull & holding

the sound of hair like   a   muffled bell we take   a
person with   us in a   little body-bag our bag that
is our body carry   a   person around the corner of

an elbow beyond the   bend   of a knee tra   velling
people form long   queue(s) up each others' arms   a per
son is com   posed of marching bones tiny   on a

cheek many calcium compo   nents clothed in the froth
of blood & skin to inter   view a person plug   their tong
ue into the lost heart shape be   hind the wardrobe in the

war   drobe a dark space with two   arms & legs & he
ad & hands like cracks   in the ceiling is there feel   the
pre   sence of a cert   ain name under the   name is the

shape of a life palp   it   ating

71

II

a mass hiss   & scrape of leg   gish poss
ibles a thorax   of brown & gold vibrating

to the sun's   gong a crowd   of ants voting
with leaves will   take the river of names in

to the rot antennae & wa   vering smells unc
oiling tongues plunged   into the   reaction

chambers of   flowers the scritch   sound of
beetle claws on   glass a nimble   wasp buzz a

kno   wing hum in the woo   den heart a scur
ry of colour & rough   parts a swarm of bony

& shiny mouths on   legs wings   of faint gho
st-stuff throw   the air over man   dibles with

sharp gui   tar like parts sl   owly crunch into
the hull of a   plant or rip   through the ruined

house of a dead d   og in   sects take the last &
first parts of all   lives the forg   otten in the bott

om of the well smells are   lifted by bees' smiles
the eye like a dome of water drop   lets wobbling

feels the w   or   ld   as if it an egg   hatched from

III

h   ung in the fr   ame of clothes a ma   ss hi
ss & sc   rape trouser-aligned & s   hirt of legg
ish possibles hel   d a voice   to make a tho

rax of brown   & gold lungs leak   out vibr

ating to the sun's go   ng with world of   ten a
crowd of ants   voting hat ringing a skull with
leaves holding the sound of a rive   r of

names names in   to the hair like a muf

fled bell antennae & wavering bell rot we take a
person with smells uncoiling   tongues us in a
little body-bag plun   ged into the re   action our

bag that is our   body chambers of flowers carry

a person a   round scritch sound a   beet   le claws
the corner of an el   bow the nimble   buzz of an elb
ow on glass beyond the bend   of knee of wasp

a knowing hum travelling   people   from in the

wooden heart long queue   up each others' scurry
-colours & rough   parts a person   is a composed
swarm marching bones   tiny mouths many calcium

-faint ghost-stuffs on a ch   eek components clothed

in air over mandible froth   of bloods & sk   in on
sharp guitar parts   interv   iew a person plug   their
slow crun   ch into the hull tongue   into lost plant rip

through heart shape behind   the ru   ined house of

dead in the wardrobe dog   insects take the last the
first part of   all lives a dark space   with two arms
& legs & head forgotten   in the bottom hands

like cracks in the well-smells are lifted ceilings are

there feel by   the bees'   smiles the presence of a
certain eye like dome of   water under the name
is dr   oplets wobbling feel the shape of   life a life

a palpitating world as if it were an egg hatched from

sweet blossom smacked
with shelved dust

musk silence snapped

The Ea(r) Tre(e)

I

a tiny the   atre of bone cut o   pen on the north
corner wind & rain of   saying can now pour in
to the bony orn   ament of cupped space an aud

ience of   silent see-throughs sits   below a cartil
age stage ten   don curtains flutter as a ran   ge of
godly weathers interr   upts a show of dram   atic ani

mals not written nor   acted ever nor never   will
be as moisture shines up the interior of a bony box
ea   ch tiny bone brick of   the the   atre's exterior is

lin   ked by a silver nerve to a   split spot lit   wound
stage-centre a ga   ping hole in the theatre's frame is
taking in   a   whole nation of st   urdy gestures gest

ures are cla   ttering along the theatre's statues stat
ues still as wind c   aught on film a vast so   liloquy o'
dry thought is being   lit stage left   just as the nor

thern corn   er he   al(l)s over

74

II

a chan   nel of soft sound fl   esh pulls in a musi
cal cloud way takes a no   ise circuit from a tree

horizon or fr   om stone imple   ments tapped ag

ainst syna   ptic shock loads the round   ness of a
spore cochlea in a jun   gle of a b   rain's design

the bones t   ools in a worksh   op of tiny not

ation strung out as birds on a fence's electric pulse
a side of a head   as an um   brella a side of a he

ad has a fin   gerless hand flattened by the mass

of sou   nd a little shov   el on a head's side a pink
inward corri   dor filling with trick   ling air & hairs

stuck in waxy argum   ents or brightening stars perf

orating a ring tremble this why   all songs swirl why
there are not straight lines of   poetry this the wh

irl pool of flesh with the inevi   table brain-end ab

                    yss

III

a tiny the   at   re of bone-s   oft sound a channel

of tin   y t   heat   re cut open the   north flesh it
pulls in corner wind and musical cloud-way rain of

sayings can now take a noise circu   it pour into the

75

bony form a tree-ho   rizon or   nament of cupping
from stone   implements an audience tapped against

synaptic space silent sea   -trough shock loud round

ness below the cart   ilage stage of the spore the coch
lea tendon curtains fl   utter as in brain jungle bones

a range of god   ly weather de   signs interrupts a show

of dramatic tools in a work   s   hop animals not writ
ten nor tiny not   at   ion strung out acted ever nor ne

ver as birds on a fen   ce   be as moisture shine elect

ric pulse up the inter   ior of bony head box each tiny
bone brick umbrell   a the the   a   tre's exterior head is

fingerless linked by a silver n   erve to flattened h   and

spilt spot lit wound-mass of sound a lit   tle centre a gap
ing hole s   hovel on   a side the   pink inward in the the

atre frame is head corrid   or filling with trickling nat

ion taking in whole air   &   hairs stuck in waxy sturdy
gestures the gestures   air & hairs   stuck arguments

of brighte   ning clattering along the th   eat   re's sta

tues the statures stars per   forating ring as still wind
caught tremble   this is why   all songs swirl on film's

vast soliloquy no   straight lines of dry (th)ought being

lit stage   left as poet   ry is a whirl   pool's north
ern corner of fl   esh where a   byss's inevitable brain

-end heals over

ground written sky
exclaiming moves hut

planet can't

Bell Feeding

hum sung on   air via bronze   a song
of light shatters slow   speed through
bones & distant   ice alike even a sea
bottom vibration is   hear   in today's
room as   bong longs   to escape and
stay all in   one   we will be pulled in

side out and in   our singing selves out

of   our crying   flesh a heat   & cold
of sound com   pressed stretched as one
long drop of bronze peels away to cent
re   's near & far   and all f   ears beg
in ground's mineral   modes   the choir
of iron is killed on   the lady of bronze

                    throats

•

a sight of bells

eyeball of   bronze a seeing   of tongues hats
of gods' hung on crosses in steep   les(s) or fall
en in a found   ers' loam rust of ringing thick

on a   waist harsh round   a mouth a   sub
mersible container of air falls th   rough ocean
a man of clapper breathing each bong   watcher

bronze loo   king down ground & up god's smelt
-misty   skirts a sound   bow is wide a crown
high a waist tight as a grieving mother's throat

       the dull bronze is brown

•

a smell of bells

hot bronze punch to nose burnt metal twists slicey
stink a hard   pong of mine   ral cry   stal man
ipulated by   heat & men &   god the fragrance

of   noise hangs   at a b   rain   stem encasing
memories with vib   rating shiny lattices that rust
round a   de   sire a snif   fing   bell pulls all

sweet smells off   sky earth   into its cavity clang
s out   existings' stinks   in our instant   stretched
beyond snouts of dogs or   sh   arks after blood in

  vast's blue no   stril of o   cean gong   going

•

a feel of bells

a chip-tuned soundbow like a   chop
piness of fro   zen sea leaves   a green

rub in   grained a cold weight of bron
ze conducts a voy   age of nerve &

soul put   your hand against a banged
metal and resonance   drains along your

finger b   ones up into a sudden wo   b
b   ling dome of   your   skull a wasp

sting ring fires its   wind   ing in   to the
flesh b   ell of your ear if   you put your

tongue on a   still bell   a meal of futures'
ch   imes pulls your taste buds out and cl

        angs t   hem with grace

 •

a sound of bells

an ear   ache of bronze list   ens out   wards with its
trumpet   shell a sea()ring ear   of bronze pouts out

stretched   shout a clapper   is a dying flower wash
ed back & forth in a fast   tide of noise a hard old dan

delion head clouted for   ever inside a clown's blo
wing   nose a hose   of vibration sits in a nozzle

of loss finds   a founder's mind &   arms drenches
a craft with forevers' measured ring rites' or wrongs'

        bronzed ong   songs

 •

fin   ger bones rin   ging a   waste a harsh round mouth
you put your tongue in   submersible container of ear with

vibrating shi   ning lattices ocean rusts   round a desire each
bong wat   ching sweet smells of a sky looks d   own into a

cavity of clangs in   stant stretched beyond god's smelt skirts
a grieving mother   after blood in vast bronze chip-tuned   ear

ache trum   pets outwards like a chopped frozen searing ear of
sea leaves green rubbing clapper sh   outs conduct voyage dying

flower of was   hed nerve & soul a fast tide of noise resonance
drains along a hose of your skull a w   asp sting vibration sits in

a nozzle loss finds a founder's flesh bell ear ring of bronze ocean

sound's lone roof
itself no kitchen

thing thoughts wrestle

moon's light of halves
house through person's vast

Mind Will

wind th   rives in sky's grasp the   wind
ing of cloth pulls   the sky's hear   t open

and takes the p   ush of clouds & distant
land into the text   ure of corn's matt talk

we pick up bun   dles of air and fee   d
them down our thr   oats while stung strings

of breeze unravel against rotating blades of
cloth laugh   ter a miller is gig   gling with

his girl in the stubble as bird   song grinds
away at sky's edges fra   ying the wind imp

      risoned in a sharp little beak

•

tight lip   ped pert pro   gress sp   rung he
aped eyes & speechless bee   tles with golden

coats put   your fingers amongst earth's cur
rency feel trickle of mol   ten dryness & brisk

itching take solid   verbs with you in the hems
of your skirts or the turned   -up furrows at the

bottoms of your trou   sers each parcel   of butt
ered day is en   graved with a soft slit of Egyp

tian sur   render to the grave's promise of spur
ting green through a   dream of forever eating

    the soil & water tor   ments of our Earth

•

cogs   kiss in orange wooden   dim mesh a
dream of tree with   an act   ual stone thought

of   now ripple   of torque & mercury   swift
thrust of grind en   gages like a child's sudden

pain again   st fingers or knees stumbling
tumbling ratchet mom   ents bang & sc   uff

wor   kings of c   lock time in   to an o
range trea   cle of clicks & hot   fric

tion harassed an()noun()cements   one
voic(ego)ingthroughthemill sm   ashed

•

the s   ound of soil's longing is white & fine
& speck   led with clots of fibrous   know

ledge take the sift   ed kisses of sun and put
your tongue against dry   sudden silk then

glue sure swelling of bread's bedclothes &
white pill   ow honest sleep   dust the air   is

a wave   lengthy frenzy of spec   kling pho
tons & filtered decibels   held in a fluid mat

rix of flour air   borne & ec   static as a god
dess's first glance at her own white white hair

•

wind   thrives in sky's tigh   t lipped pert
progress the winding   of cloth pulls heaped
eyes & speech   less beetles sky's heart open

with golden   coats take the push of cloud's
fingers amongst earth   corn's mat-talk molten
dryness & itch pick   up bundles of air take

solid verbs with you in your   hems feed them
down our throats your skirts or the turn-up fur
rows while stung   breeze st   rings bottoms of

your trousers unravel against the rotating parcel
of buttered day blades   of laughing cloth engra
ved with a soft   slit the mill   er   is giggling

with Egyptian   surrender his girl in the stubble
as the graves promise of spurting bird   song
grinds away at green through   dream the edges

of sky and the wind of for   ever eating the soil
is a sharp little beak impris   oned in water torm
ents of Earth cogs kiss in orange wooden sounds

of soil's longing   dim mesh a dream   of tree
white & fine & speckled   with an actual stone
thought clots   of fibrous knowledge now   the

ripple of torque & sifted kisses for   sun mercury
-swift   thrust your ton   gue against dry grind
engages   like a ch   ild's   sudden silk sudden

new pain against the swelling of b   read's bed cl
othes fingers   & knees stumbling in white pillow
honest sleep   dust tumbling ratchet moments   air

wave   lengthy fren   zy bang & scu   ff a working
of speckling photons & fil   tered clock-time into
orange sound vibration h   eld in a treacle of clicks

hot friction-flu   id matrix of fl   our air   borne
haras   sed announcements one   & ecsta   tic as a
Rap   unzel's first vo   ice going through the mill

-smashed glance at her w   hite w   hite h   air

clothes' aligned voice gold

soot from shadow fell naked
writhes cradling cloud

add hut's choir

Pwloraky

I

her spinning-top eyes his   die mind she
sets talk rolling & he catches   her with
his hop   marble hearts clack &   the rules

get broken abruptly   they re-write the man
ouvres he   begins   to ladder her snake-place
& tip   the wheels of her song she   begins

by elasticated mouthing of rhymes & hand
clap clasps the rope   comes tight   between
them & the skip   of life begins an end   his

brand-new toy gleams her   old toy is dull
the 2   are grabbed greedily smashed mixed
into the   one   gleaming rusty thing   bits

of old & new fascinate a third player   who
will heap this toy on his desk until   his throat
produces squeals of a   child from a future

II

fingery billhooks chat   together about cut
twigs & red   sap they chat   along the hedge

line all day the hammer on the roof clatters at
the house's   skin the man   with nails in his

mouth sweats attentions   like the whole plunging
sun's grief until   evening brings gleeful boxes of

packed day   the carpenter slides honesty across
grain and the bite of his wit   shaves away light

and lets   coils of day gather by his boots   the
ploughman's bent spanner tingles in his palm he

torques the bolts on the bright   soil-fish his heart
pushes and horse   pulled   through brown sea by

day's end each tool is deepened   slightly   by hands
that've sweated for   set   pieces of survival   arrive

III

her spinning-top eyes & his dice fingers & billhook chat
together   mind   she set the talk rolling and he about cut

twigs & red sap they caught   her with his hop marble chat
along the hedgeline   all day   heart clacked and the rules

broke the hammer   he begins the ladder   her snake in his
mouth sweats tip   the wheels of her song   like the whole

plunging sun grieving elastic   mouthing of evening brings
gleeful boxes of rhymes & hand clap clasps pack day the car

penter slides   rope   comes tight between them & honesty
across the grain   the skip of life begins the bite of his wit

shaves away the brand new   toy gleams light coils of day
gather by old dull toy   the two were his boots the   plough

man's bent spanner smashed by greed re-mixes into tingles
in his palm as he talks a   gleaming rusty thing bits   of

bolt in the bright soil fish his heart old   & new fascinating
the player & horse pull through   the sea of who would   keep

this toy on his brown by day's end each   tool on his desk his
throat produces is slightly deepened by the hands' squeal   a

child in the future has sweated for set   pieces   of arrival

room of spectacular roads' here

Ho Use Goneg Rows

jig's wit-possible broken   over distance throws

dice down on   to grasses & stones
the verge is audience   grass feels mice
said need   to rebreak again's   gains

pick a place   to place each open

houseless ground upon   as cats' eyes spread
thin gazes over knolls   a mountain path has been
pulled by afraid beings   stuck in a city canyon

want land's   surround-embrace   see executives adding
with stones   flick out to fend
for selves   the telephone box is full   of meat & cutlery try

gaining later   repeat down roadsides   for hunger follows

where movement's   chrysalis grows spread
some self beyond its corner   in a cold-air-close
self's dense speck   the road's surface warmed

by known screams   a pavement remains

                    as cold as a sky   a first footstep
                    topples a tower   but is a faint
                    last footprint   under moss

the loyal sky   comforting a river

whilst furred turds wait   huge space like a
mind off ground   like so very much afraid
of wanting to throw   dice down

thorns & puss   on a road's surface

every animal ever taken   by a road's surface
possible is broken less   over home's distance so
a chrysalis of movement's   house grows

Sheidek

I

put the shape   away begin   the distance of other we
located our   place of forgotten the chosen   no place

is existing with   out us you were far   off near   to

the war   drobe tucked under the board across an ocean
list   en   to the creaking as feet approach don't   breathe

out and the dust's treachery   will   not swirl it is for
bidden to be   gindis   covery   in the seclusion you

may start memory loss on the other   hand   a whole house
vanished she began   by making   a map of the corner

she got bricked into the map   was intricate by following
the map she located her loss was   able   to paint & polish

it so its beauty pushed   her deeper   into the corner her
husband   never suspects the deeds of the skirtingboard

all yesterday   yes   to dust

91

II

she lets her hands   free they go all   up&down
unseen textures they   drag her body be   hind

as they meticulously   road rid ride   lost ground
her   nails pick at every splinter   or hiss of scurf

she just lets her whole   touch-factory prod   uce
possibilities of location the   man watching   could

not tell   what   was   happening his eyes   were
tunnels that visual info travels   down   through but

no sense could mix with   is   with his cave brain
the light of one   thought glimmers   in the cave

of him the pressure   of this light dents the deep
tangled texture of ground her   hands madly go along

her hand-pause   she feels this light   -press sure
an even & smooth   dent   tiny but distinct   ink

amongst raucous obstacles bristling against
her sweetly finger   printed probes   robes rob

III

she lets her hands begin   the distance we   lo
cated our place of un   seen textures the chosen no
place dragged her body without us   you   were

far and meticulously rode the lost ground off near
to the wardrobe just tucked nails   picking at every
splinter under the board across an   ocean   of scurf

she just let her whole   feet approach touch-factory
produce the man   watching could dust treachery's
location   it is   forbidden to wear tunnels   disc

ovary in the sec   lusion you travelled through memory
loss on the other mixed   his cave brain she of one
thought gleams a whole   house vanished in the cave

of him making a map of the other pressure this light
dented beauty   pushed light pressure into the corner
tiny but distinct fingerprinted probes of   yesterday

                        's skirtingboard

to angle runes
with semantics' world

blank *than*

birch scratches make mind

Light's Senses
after Zoë Childerly's & Peter Rumney's *Absence of*   *Light*

a silve   red fox crouches in   tent   on empty illuminated
locks the ill   icit wit   nest   said unseen quarry on a plain

wooden chair sir   rounds   a con's eaten-out ark   hunt the
sitter gone   a brook dark by darkness's vaguely lit lane &

den hair   ties   beyond into knotted   night met   allic etch
plated vixen   illu   mined by localised   branches the chair

is round anchors   led   by a pale homemade light   cooling
hot wire   & tiny woodland put together with tweezers   rot

ting lunar vag   rant of watching splashed   smooth machined
varnished timber con   trasts natural   rasps strong   shadows

        if   as a grotto of pre   cise breath held like oil

House by Tent

I's world   -walls flap as reflective   wind
rushes its   sliding shines inside through   child

hood shaped chinks in   wet cloth I   conducts

a red   brick   -pulling   each plug of solid   c
licks and   memories g   lug like   a dog's lapp

ing at a solution of night deeds   moments a body

int   erupts space   dissolved in   feathery mil
dew-stinking urges the wind   blows and   the big

old house gently creaks   whilsts   the tent is a mass

of rabid cloth digesting a little   boy & his pictures
of nudes   :   trees with mud   dy holes & wick

ed dew

air will sacrifice vowels

clear dead window
heat's space a glacier

nothing lonely

back – to oak – words

meadow   a soil child's a against open
moments breaking gently   ripples of
rattles   soft & plhuff   makes makes

child a loss   solid thrown   each
time through rain   by built   been
throat   a throat   a that's pool   a

in lost   each pebbles in throws   mouth
this by child   a crown snakes still   plate
root   meadow opened   down blown

oak   child a soil   meadow's a against

Their Tree

She sights the tree between
two huge derelict distribution sheds.
It stops

her as if her husband
suddenly lived again.

A spring oak on the horizon –
mature with dark thick twisting limbs
holding fresh mists of greenery.

If she could remember the word,
she'd utter – *miracle*. Her children

only know trees as myths.

It's as if the tree
is balanced

        on a wire
        stretched
        between

two hollow memorials.

See how she wants so much –
wants to keep the tree.

      She puts her nearly-see-through hand
      up to the horizon, and cups the tiny oak.
      It is impossible to speak of, but
      the perfect miniature tree roots
      itself into her palm – roots through
      her veins, and feeds gently on her blood.

      She & her stick-children are in awe
      of the oak standing up from her hand.
      The light is sprinkled on its leaves as if
      green moth-dust clothed it.
      And that fresh ancient scent of deep green.
      Radiant green again. They weep.

      Her son & daughter moan,
      then yell no words. But

      their breaths shake
      the little oak's limbs. It sways.
      And the roots, as they take
      the strain and move
      in her flesh,

      hurt.

grime perception goes on tiny
near hands over made memories

that folded smell grass gleaming

Fast Gain Vales
translated from Harriet Tarlo's *slow*   *riddles*

unlike   water throwing earth   dull depth
after   denying float   unlike   a change
where the wasp louds predictably   I don't

know   I am deaf   unlike   a bud core
throwing masses   of green   the time

when leaves will

Stories of Sward

translated from   Alison Croggon's *Songs of Grass*

a glove's genius   gesticulation   showed us a
fiction of its handless   coupling   on a cropped

hush   now a mouse crawls numerous backbones
of fescue   above sombre soil that   spades her

away skywards through   her   density today's

sward is green and   vociferous apart   from the
wilting yellow   blade   in its brain   thinking

today & today

Selfy Gardenish Time

grass fractures   sunlight a garden   is a mouth & my
footsteps grow across old cool green it is   a tree to a
left that watches me   most a cedar is   a wardrobe of

young souls hah rhododendrons   have dragons' eyelids
and a pigeon in a button   -hole of an even   ing recites
what I'd like to   think in low blow   n tones   notes

birdsong is a cla   shing of moons & stars organ   ised
and oiled by a ghost's living   bits grass is   text vertical
verses of green in rows   dried grass's a miniature nation's

remains   a neat hay smell of these remn   ants if un-mini
aturised would ex   pand to a bit   ter   vastness paving
stones are seg   ments of th   ick skin   shed by a history

of mowing to a   right is pulling   up blades of light and sn
apping a moment across a t   own's back foxgloves   speak
a deep tunnel's forgotten   smells ivy   is a desire for cloth

mag   nified thous   ands of times something   virile sighs
and rasps through grass like a growing rash and wraps round
a godly grayle that was lost and left on a metal bench in a fa

101

mous dead man's childhood den a white table   & chairs feel
someone else's   stillness it is not an insect's   decision it is
not a fox's it   is mine a birdbath   is a place of ruin for rain's

p   roofs of nothing   so

Prin Tutter

I

tree   part & bird   claw blackened on   sheen we
take each cr   iss of a solid ou   tside & lace cro

sses to curls or   spikes to ovals each   tip of a
black cut stitched on birch   is a tip   of shall   ow

deep we are a lace   of   dark on light water we
spread our over   page like   a nation in ranks

escaping or a herd   of org   an   ised animals travel
ling from one   notion to an   other notion each slash

in a mud or gouge through   ice lines up a thought
to mate   rial vibrat   ions paint a rock with paws &

prints trouble a ground   from   skies' high mouths

II

air animal   tightened ag   ainst flesh chords   air
vibrated by roar folds &   eating parts clouds   of
sound weathering a soul out   in   to a() ear's house

ea   ch deci   bel fel   t by hate or love st   retched a
cross infinity's tiny orifice so   a world & beyond gongs
from creature whilst lungs coagulate in a chest's crack

103

listen to an   ants' feet or hawks' wings rub   sky pull
a fee   ling of these out   of your cathedral throat and
let go   ats of words casc   ade down molecular stairs

into others' ears to cry   stallise blood's the   sis

III

tree-part & bird claw tightened   against animal air
we flesh chords blackened on   sheen take each criss

of a roar   folds by eating   solid outside & lace crosses
parts   clouds of sound to curls   to spikes to   ovals

wea   thering from a soul each   tip of a black   out
into a(n) (l)ear's house each decibel felt   by cut stitched

on birch a tip of shallow(   )deep we hate or lv strtchd
a lace of dark across infinity's tiny orifice   a world

beyond light   water we spread gongs from   creatures
out over a page   like a nation lungs coagulate in

ranks escaping chest's crack-listen   her   ds of organised
anim   als travelling   from one notion to   an ant's

feet to another notion each   hawk wing rubs sky slash
in a mud or gouge   pull a feeling of these out   of your

cathedral throat-ice   lines up a thought   material
vibrations let goats   of words a rock   with paws &

prints cascades down molecular trouble   a ground
from stairs into   other's ears sky's   high mouth

crystallises bloo   dy faeces

A Box of Badger-Time

a black/white stripe-kiss   pine
-needle wishes   hard green regretted

acorns   beetle statistics   a box
of fibrous thoughts   coarse

as star-glass   scratchy as snapped
bone   mass gass viral impasse

fast spit-stabs   yap-yap-yap   four
brown walls badgers claw   trees

nails in a copse-box   nails
a boar may piss against   his

high-pitched hot shit   a box
of woodland smell-shouts   a ribbon

of tarmac

Reak Wald

I

foot   to path to   core of soil dark to   spl   ice of lit
cloud edge foot against   crag-edge   foot along   ot(   )her

feet creeping through slats in a glass   y sound sm   ashed
wood   land near tw   irling sea foot   down & foot

across knee splays open   to horizons aching limb you
& me take   feet away with our   breaths(') thump of gravity

& the smoke of dist   urbed dust souls a step follows a step a
hold all   ows breaks places to   begin & end in as sun over

throws   stars & stars   trickle along the big   leg bones of
hum   an passages a footpath has feet in   touch has feet kept

in a nar   row groove   has landscape placed away from tread
the foot on the foot   path the growth   of trail a journey's bloo

m pushing its frag   rance across a surface   on a rock round a
lava core   in a space   full of tiny white   hot foot   prints

        cast across a deep   black walk   less void

II

eyes pat ag   ainst   specks flicks
of place en   ter nerve sayings pr

inted parts   of heart or   tree gath
er mom   ent   um in a   lens's

condensation pick   up on crossed
twigs   snapped vowel lit   on a pine

cone sniff   at the spore   of a boo
k's meal feel   a rough trace a

page   leaves   behind on the floo
r of a crea   ture's mind open *the*

first bir   d-shape with your mouth
then twist the second snapped twig

with your   ears this   string of little
sig   nals spilt   into the grass   and

cl   inging to ru   nning beasts is w
here   a story's nerves un   ravel and

you can begin to pass beyond   *the*
white bound   ary of paper brain (*t*)*his*

fo   otpr   int is a bird's *this*   scrape
is a man   's inj   ured foot a curly ch

ain of inky movements is broken being
men   ding a world with letter &

ph()one( )me   this is not going
to be   lit by fire it   's go   in   g to

crack & cr   aze ice smashed by a met
eorite ea   ch read word is   convul

            sin   g b   east

III

foo   t to path to core   of eyes pat
against specks soil   dark to splice
of lit flicks of   place enter   nerve

cloud   edge foot against sayings'
printed parts   crag-edge   foot
a   long other   heart of tree gather

moment(-)feet creeping through slats
in a lens's conden   sation in a sma
shed glassy sound   pick   up on *the*

crossed twigs   *the*   snapped hiero
glyph of woodland near twirling sea
splattered vow   el lit on a foot down

& foot across pine gone sniff a knee
's sp   lay to horiz   on aching limbs
you & me   take spore of a book's

meal feel feet   away with our breaths
a rough   trace a page   leaves thump
of gravity & smoke behind   a floor a

creature's mind disturbs dust souls first
bird-sh   ape your mouth-step   follow
a step a   hold then taste *the*   second

snapped allows breaths' places to beg
in an end a   sun overth   rows twig
with ears'   stars and stars   trickle a

long little signals   split big leg bones
of human grass clinging to running a
footpath beast is   where   a story

passages feet   in touch have nerves
unravel feet kept in a narrow groove
begintopassbeyondwhiteboundary of

paper brain has landscape placed   a
way from tre   ad the foot on this foot
path is a bird's foot   path following

a foot on scrape is a man's injured *the*
footpath   a growth of   foot this
curly chain a journey's bloom   push

es in   ky movements a broken trail fra
grance across a   surface being mending
a letter on rock round lava with worlds

and pho   nemes cure in a space full
is not   going   to be lit by   fire it   is
going to craz &   crake like tiny white

hot footprint   s cast across a   deep
black ice smashed   by   a meteo
rite each read   word   is convulsing

        beasts' walkless void

light cracks fields
home as histories

ring that time's breath

Rildoute Werness

I

possible br   oken o   ver distance reass
embled out of   sight broken   when you ar

rive again the grasses & stones the   run
ning deer the mouse just   to your left they

all break a pos   sible & inst   antly make it
better to rebreak again & ag   ain like spli

ntered bone just a   fter a lion bit like open
houseless gr   ound going on over   the

hinge with s   pace like y   our hear   t sp
read so th   in   it cove   rs each knoll & em

pty grass tract l   ike wanting so very mu
ch but being   afr   aid to want a land surro

unds and embraces flicks   you out to find you
rself you   're all bli   sters & (t)horns & puss as

hunger follows   you it is   a stone a leaf h
unger in your hair you spread   self to each corn

110

er of end   less you are a dense   speck screams
of the knowing the furred & four   legged egg

you out of m   anness a   sky floats on land a land
is wider than e   very breath taken by every an

imal ever and beyond that sky's stars some   one
is in   a   city but   the   (c)ity is gone there

is a top   pled tower faint   under moss there
is a ben   t aerial more home to crows than signa

ls a sky is flo   ating a river land is floating on caves
you are floating your   own breath distance sinks

an on   ly escape to foll   ow a fall

II

spl   it lane movem   ent my jig white lined   I brink
(b(ring)link)   my   want in orange begin   to throw

d   ice down a wayahead a verge   is audience all grass
will feel a me pass a you said thought   was the tarmac

over love's earth   a you said a   we needs a car boots
are not sw   ift enough a we pick   a place to place ea

ch foot a you said it is t   ime for ABC gas & brake &
spinning fr   iction discs a car'   s eyes are all he   aped

in a corner of a()round   about the northern park has bee
n pulled off its ground and   stuck in a city can   yon see

an executive adding stones to cairns a telephone box &
tele   graph poles re   peat down ro   adsides beca   use

travel is blinks a kind of mu   shiness where the chrysalis
of movement grows arrivals hug   e & furry a cold air close

to a road surface war   med by passing rubber revolving a c
old air on a pave   ment remains   cold as boots or shoes mo

ve through it a dog turd waits it   is so   sha(r)p(e)ly cut so
spicily ann   ounced in summer slips   into sandals to grease

travels' toes a first foot   step is a point of take and a last a
point of taken a   motion some giving of sw   eat to dust a

loyal path winds round ground an adult   erous road tunnels

III

      j   ig white   possibles broken o
      ver distance reassem   bled split

lane movement lined one blink want in o   range
begin the grasses & stones the running deer throw

      dice down waya   heads a mouse
      just to left they all break verge au

dience all grass w   ill feel a possible instantly make it
a better said thought was a tar   mac to rebreak aga   in

      & aga   in like splinte   red over loves'
      earth said need bone just af   ter li   on

bit like a car bo   ots are not swift eno   ugh to open hous
eelse ground going on over pick a place to place each foot

      a 'the' huge space like   art said it's ti
      me for ABC gas & b   rake spread so thin

cover each k   no   ll's spinning friction disc cats' e   yes
are emp   ty grass tracts like wanting all heaped in a round

about's corner so very much but   being
afraid about mountain p   arks pulled

want land surrounds and embraces off its ground stuck   in
city c   an   yon flicks out to find selves see executives ad

ding stones to all b   listers north &
puss cairns telep   hone box & teleg

raph hunger follow   it is   a stone pole repeats d   own road
side because it is a leaf   in hair travel blinks a kind moth   in

ess spreads each corner's arrival
huge & furry cold air close end

less dense speck to toad's surface warmed by creams no   wing
furred passing of rubber revolving cold air & fore-l   egged egg

out of m   anness on a pave   ment's re
mains cold   as   sky floats on (l)and

wilder than every breath boots & shoes move through dog taken
by very animal ever turd waiting   so s   harply cut beyond sky's

stars some so   spicily announced in sum
mer it is in a   city but city   gone will slip

into sand   als to grease a toppled toe's faint tower travel's first
foot   fall faint under moss there   is an aerial's point of t   ake

& a last foots   tep is more home
to crows th   an signal point tak

en motion is some sky floating on river giving sweat to dust's loy
al land is floating on lack path wind round ground floating   own

broken distance adulterous
road tunnels sink on   ly's

e   scape to fall   ow foal

corn moon bonds
a coin's bend

small mouth vast air

A Gap, a Construct Town, an   English Edge
after artist & retoucher Helen Saunders' *Constructed Cities* & *Constructed Landscapes*

a cob   web a   (cr)oss   a sub   way lamp greasy
moisture seeping   from bricks a skip   full
of thoughts empty of

                 selves clean gleaming

metallic car   paint a roof   of a   build
ing reflected   in a sh   all   ow puddle   on
concrete pass   beneath *the* railway   to a

sky holding a mile in its arms a gap   in a

wire   mesh fence barbed   wire   gritty with
rust an orange   dumper truck its   engine chu   g

ging a trickle &   crump of its
load dumped an   ocean   edge seep
ing in   to scrap   metal a track to

wards a mountainous heap of
earth a girl   sat on *the*

white tip   of a lock   gate's
lever distant rain's grey

matter   congeals to dream   a puddle half

         way a   long

Nown

house crum   bles along a road its p   arts
fil   ter down through ground win   dow pow
der mingles with gold in river songs it is not

to   be be   lieved the way a roo   f can take

to ea   ting all the homes in e   very eye when
I   was a house   I   held my cell   ar it was
not un   til I fell in love with   the wind & the

dan   cing tree in my gard   en that I de

served the silver of my window entire sky kept
safe by a way   side as clouds tied to glo   ries(')
moi   sture(s) along a dry road's left side where cr

umbling house parts sound out

lamp at evening

listen

alive shed against roaring

Disturbance
translated from part of
Peter Dent's *Settlement*

there is not more to be heard
than can't be heard   many

dim-lit rough faces
on a self-dumb but remarkable

large rock   listening
to old occasion   to others' selves

another night or just this night
breezeless   the doldrums

meadow of matter   of chooses
dimming heading abroad

beyond found   so listening
there after we ignore

do we forget others' selves?
a new perfect semiology

crystallised   to which yes nothing
yes may un-address

distances   whose shades
will disturb for the time

nothing of a
which hasn't to be labelled

trees' buds and a first red drop
yes them to be opaque   their something

the disclosure to be (given
yes ledgers action) disturbed

under computer-close   the blurred
data of others' soaked and dissolved

as one certain stair
a thousand steps up breaks

down   a pagan rune
to dark

round a gleaming
of colliding round

one's bones

one of other

Acknowledgements

Some of the poems (or versions of them) have been previously published in the following magazines, to whose editors I am grateful:

Broken Compass, Dusie, Fire, Neon Highway, Raunchland, Shadowtrain, Shearsman, Stride, Tears in the Fence, Under The Radar.

I am grateful to Radio Wildfire for online-broadcasting sound-enhanced versions of *Fice* and *The Ea(r) Tre(e)*.

Moving was commissioned in 2005, by Leicester's Phoenix Arts.

The third part of *Biscuits Thrown From a Window* was commissioned by curator John Clark, and exhibited at Sheffield Hallam University's End Gallery in March 2007. *Biscuits Thrown From a Window* is the title of a short performance film by artist Dave Ball.

I am grateful to the following people, for critical comment and/or encouragement relating to individual poems or the entire manuscript: David Caddy, Alison Croggon, Allan Baker, Katie Daniels, Peter Dent, John Clark, Chris Jones, Kerry Featherstone, Rob Hamberger, Jeremy Hilton, Brian Lewis, Rupert Loydell, Helen Mort, Ian Seed, Simon Perril, Peter Rumney, Helen Saunders, Gavin Stewart, Harriet Tarlo, Pam Thompson, Michael Tolkien, Deborah Tyler-Bennett.

As ever, thank you to Julia Thornley for her close critical attention to the manuscript, and for her precision proof reading.

Thank you to Tony Frazer for his careful and creative attention towards *House At Out*'s layout.

Thank you to my partner Nikki Clayton for her continuing to drive our attempts to dwell, imagined or otherwise… indoors or out…

Lightning Source UK Ltd.
Milton Keynes UK
UKOW02f2314211015

261141UK00001B/82/P